Fighting for Reproductive Justice

Fighting for Reproductive Justice

Black Women Leading a Movement

Ngeri Nnachi

LERNER PUBLICATIONS ◆ MINNEAPOLIS

To my dearest Nnenna, a.k.a. Mini Me,
May you continue to harness the power that you and I share for good and continually grow into the brightly shining light that you are. Just like many of the women mentioned here, you are powerful beyond measure and I am ALWAYS so proud.

Copyright © 2024 by Lerner Publishing Group, Inc.

All rights reserved. International copyright secured. No part of this book may be reproduced, stored in a retrieval system, or transmitted in any form or by any means—electronic, mechanical, photocopying, recording, or otherwise—without the prior written permission of Lerner Publishing Group, Inc., except for the inclusion of brief quotations in an acknowledged review.

Lerner Publications Company
An imprint of Lerner Publishing Group, Inc.
241 First Avenue North
Minneapolis, MN 55401 USA

For reading levels and more information, look up this title at www.lernerbooks.com.

Main body text set in Rotis Serif Std 55 Regular. Typeface provided by Adobe Systems.

Designer: Lauren Cooper
Lerner team: Sue Marquis

Library of Congress Cataloging-in-Publication Data

Names: Nnachi, Ngeri, author.
Title: Fighting for reproductive justice : Black women leading a movement / Ngeri Nnachi.
Description: Minneapolis : Lerner Publications, [2024] | Series: Gateway biographies | Includes bibliographical references and index. | Audience: Ages 9-14 | Audience: Grades 4-6 | Summary: "Reproductive rights have been hot-button issues for generations, and recent legal decisions have put these arguments back in the spotlight. Learn about the women of color who are leading a movement to protect reproductive rights"— Provided by publisher.
Identifiers: LCCN 2023022618 (print) | LCCN 2023022619 (ebook) | ISBN 9798765610435 (library binding) | ISBN 9798765623817 (paperback) | ISBN 9798765614662 (epub)
Subjects: LCSH: Reproductive rights—United States—History—Juvenile literature. | Women's rights—United States—History—Juvenile literature. | Minority women—Political activity—United States—History—Juvenile literature.
Classification: LCC HQ766.5.U5 N63 2024 (print) | LCC HQ766.5.U5 (ebook) | DDC 305.420973—dc23/eng/20230616

LC record available at https://lccn.loc.gov/2023022618
LC ebook record available at https://lccn.loc.gov/2023022619

Manufactured in the United States of America
1-1009628-51716-8/1/2023

TABLE OF CONTENTS

Founding the Reproductive Justice Movement 8

Spreading the Word 11

Period Poverty 14

Medical Research and Lack of Consent 15

Bodily Autonomy and Rights 19

Birth Control 23

Black Women and Birth Control 29

Abortion Rights and *Roe v. Wade* 35

Still Working for Reproductive Justice 37

Important Dates 42
Source Notes 44
Selected Bibliography 44
Learn More 46
Index 47

The National Council of Negro Women meets in 1935. Mary McLeod Bethune founded the organization, working alongside activists such as Dorothy Ferebee and Dorothy Height.

In 1943 two Black women named Mamie and Edna appeared in court in Charleston, South Carolina. They had been accused of giving illegal abortions to many of their neighbors. Then most state laws said that abortion was legal in early stages of pregnancy or if the mother's life was at risk. Women who needed abortions usually got them from their doctors, and most people seemed to agree that those doctors and their pregnant patients could make those decisions together. Laws were in place, though, that someone who helped a pregnant woman with an abortion later on in a pregnancy could be punished.

Together, Mamie and her daughter Edna helped women who needed abortions. The charges against sixty-one-year-old Mamie were that she had committed a crime against a married white woman named Stella. Stella had come to Mamie for help in ending her pregnancy. After the abortion, Stella needed further medical attention. When she received help from doctors, she told them about Mamie.

A police raid of Mamie and Edna's home found abortion instruments and printed instructions on how to perform an abortion. Historians don't know much more about this case, but Mamie and Edna may have been charged with a crime because they were Black women helping a white woman. Or maybe it was because they weren't licensed doctors. If Stella had not needed to see a doctor after the abortion, Mamie and Edna may not have had to go to court.

Founding the Reproductive Justice Movement

Reproductive justice means that people have the right to decide for themselves when and if they have children. Black women have been leading the fight for reproductive justice for generations. This included spreading information about birth control, advocating for fair and accessible health care for women of all backgrounds, and activism to make abortion safe and legal.

The 1992 March for Women's Lives drew more than three hundred thousand protesters to Washington, DC. At the time, the Supreme Court was considering a case that might have overturned *Roe v. Wade*, a landmark abortion case.

The term *reproductive justice* came from a 1994 meeting in Chicago. A group of twelve Black women had just attended a conference organized by then president Bill Clinton. It was supposed to be about how to improve health care in the United States.

But these women were not impressed by what they heard. They didn't think the conference had focused enough on services such as sexually transmitted infection tests or fibroid screenings. Both of these services impacted their community. The women also believed that parts of the conversation were missing. Nobody had mentioned that reproductive issues can be affected by how much money someone makes, by whether someone has a place to live, or even by where they live.

In their hotel room meeting, these twelve women coined the term *reproductive justice*. Reproductive justice includes the right to decide whether to have children, to make one's own health decisions, and to raise children in a safe place. These women called themselves the Women

The 2023 Women's March in Washington, DC, drew attention to the fiftieth anniversary of the Supreme Court decision in *Roe v. Wade*.

of African Descent for Reproductive Justice. They are considered the founding mothers of the reproductive justice movement.

Based on what they had heard in the Chicago conference, the women knew they needed to tell people about their misgivings. They wanted lawmakers to listen to their concerns about how Clinton's health-care reforms would harm Black women. The women worked hard to get support from hundreds of Black women around the country to advocate for health-care reforms that could benefit Black women.

Spreading the Word

To spread their message advocating for reproductive rights for all women, the Women of African Descent for Reproductive Justice collected $40,000 to pay for a historic full-page ad in the *Washington Post* newspaper a few months after the Chicago conference. Their goal was to draw attention to their concerns and ask lawmakers to focus on issues of reproductive justice.

After the ad was published, a press conference was held in Washington, DC. This ad and the press conference caught the attention of many around the country, including author Alice Walker and members of Congress Eleanor Holmes Norton, Maxine Waters, and Eva Clayton. These women supported the activists and their message by speaking at the press conference.

Congressional leaders Maxine Waters (*left front*) and Eleanor Holmes Norton share a hug at a 2009 event.

A few weeks later, these activists attended the International Conference on Population and Development in Egypt. They wanted international leaders to make it safe, legal, and easy for women around the world to find and use birth control and other family planning tools.

Other organizations have defined reproductive justice slightly differently. A wide variety of groups are working for the freedom for all women and girls to make their own decisions about what works best for them. Asian Communities for Reproductive Justice, for example, defines reproductive justice as "the complete physical, mental, spiritual, political, social, and economic well-being of women and girls." The group, founded in 1989, focuses on the reproductive health of Asian women and girls. It creates and hosts education programs to help Asian women and girls learn more about their rights.

Monica Simpson, speaking here at a 2021 rally, is the executive director of SisterSong Women of Color Reproductive Justice Collective, a collective of reproductive rights organizations.

Period Poverty

Reproductive justice includes other aspects of health as well. Every month, most female teenage and adult bodies prepare for pregnancy. Most months, no pregnancy begins, and the uterus sheds its lining through menstruation. Girls and women often use cloth or disposable materials to absorb the discharge.

But some girls around the world don't have access to these kinds of products. Not having these menstrual products is known as period poverty. Period poverty can make it hard to go to school or participate in activities. It can also cause health problems. Without access to pads or

Some women and girls don't have easy access to period products such as pads, tampons, or menstrual cups.

tampons, some people use dirty rags or leaves, which can cause infections or other medical problems.

Some girls or women may also skip meals or take medication to try to stop their periods, This can lead to medical problems such as anemia, caused by low iron levels, or unhealthy relationships with food. Other people without access to period products might feel isolated, lonely, or depressed.

One activist fighting period poverty is Yanique Brandford. As a teenager in Jamaica, she and her family made their own pads from household items such as plastic and paper. Her family later moved to Toronto, Canada, where in 2018 she created a nonprofit organization that gives menstrual products to people who need them.

Indonesian teen Alisha Triawan realized that she and her friends weren't learning much about their bodies or their menstrual health. In 2019 she started a group that educates young people about periods and gives out menstrual supplies.

Medical Research and Lack of Consent

Institutions and scientists in the United States have learned a lot about the human body over the years. But those institutions have also performed much of their medical research on people of color, especially Black women, without asking their permission.

James Marion Sims was a surgeon in Alabama in the nineteenth century. He developed a surgery to help with certain health problems that happened during childbirth. He is often called the Father of Modern Gynecology. Most historians agree that the surgery he developed was extremely helpful for women with those health problems. But they also point out that he performed all of his practice experiments on enslaved Black women without their consent and without pain medication. He believed that Black women couldn't feel pain.

In 1951 Henrietta Lacks was a thirty-year-old mother of five children. She visited Johns Hopkins Hospital in Baltimore, Maryland, after experiencing vaginal bleeding. Johns Hopkins was one of the only hospitals willing to care for lower-income African Americans. Doctors found that Lacks had cervical cancer and started radium treatments.

Johns Hopkins sent cell samples of all cancer patients to a local research lab. Other patients' cells usually died right away. But Lacks's cells multiplied. Researchers in the lab nicknamed the cells HeLa cells, for her name, and used them for decades to study diseases and improve medical treatments.

Henrietta Lacks died a few months after her initial visit to Johns Hopkins. But neither she nor her family members knew that her cells helped scientists make huge leaps in medical knowledge and treatment. The doctors who took her cell samples didn't even tell Lacks they were doing so. None of what those researchers did was illegal

Anarcha, Betsey, and Lucy

Modern medical practice would be very different without the sacrifices of enslaved Black women. In the nineteenth century, the surgeon James Marion Sims of Alabama tried out experimental new procedures on enslaved Black women. Three of these women, Anarcha, Betsey, and Lucy, suffered from a painful medical condition that affected women after a difficult childbirth. Their conditions were so painful that they couldn't work, so their enslavers "sold" them to Sims.

Sims tested new treatments on these women and others, though he likely never asked their permission. He tied them to the operating table and didn't give them pain medication during surgery, even though it was available then. He also invited other white male doctors to watch the operations. Anarcha alone went through thirty surgeries in four years.

The Mothers of Gynecology Monument in Montgomery, Alabama, honors Anarcha, Betsey, and Lucy, who suffered experimental surgeries for their health conditions.

Henrietta Lacks's grandson keeps this photo of her in his home.

at the time. But these days, using a person's cells in such a way would require their consent.

Sixty years later, a journalist researched and wrote a book about Lacks's life. A few years later, Oprah Winfrey made and starred in a TV movie based on the book.

Bodily Autonomy and Rights

The United States has a long history of people in power, who have tended to be wealthy white men, believing they have the right to make decisions about women's bodies. During the time of slavery, enslavers wanted Black women to have many children, making more people who would work for them. After slavery ended, many white people wanted to decrease the Black population.

Eugenics is the racist view that only certain people deserve to have children. In the United States, that has often meant that wealthy white people think that they deserve to have children more than anyone else. In the late nineteenth and early twentieth centuries, many powerful people believed in eugenics and made laws that reflected those beliefs.

Historically, Black women have been one of the most targeted groups of people to be sterilized without being asked first. Sterilization removes someone's ability to reproduce. For many years, Black women might have gone to a hospital for any reason, including giving birth, and been sterilized without their knowledge.

Forced sterilization has not been limited to Black women. Throughout American history, lawmakers have decided that certain people did not deserve to have children. Poor people, women of color, and those with disabilities have all been sterilized without their consent. The US Supreme Court ruled in 1927, for instance, that it was okay for a mental health institution to sterilize all its patients, with or without their consent.

In 1960 North Carolina created a voluntary sterilization law. This law made it legal to remove someone's ability to have children if they received welfare. This government program helps support people who can't afford basic needs, such as food or housing. Some lawmakers believed that anyone on welfare could not afford children and would be better off without them. So a person who needed help had to agree to sterilization to qualify for that help.

In North Carolina alone, seventy-six hundred people were forcibly sterilized between 1929 and 1973. This happened to Black women far more often than to white women or white men. In the 1960s and 1970s, more than one hundred thousand Latina, Indigenous, and Black women were forced into sterilization.

In 1964 Mississippi activist and community leader Fannie Lou Hamer protested a sterilization bill passed by the House of Representatives. The bill would fine or imprison unmarried women who had children, and Hamer believed it targeted African American women. If women did not want to pay a fine or go to prison, they could choose to be sterilized. Most white male lawmakers thought that women should only have children if they were married to men. If they were not, those men believed, the women were not capable of making good decisions.

This was not the only way that Black women were being sterilized. Hamer herself had been sterilized without her knowledge after surgery to remove a fibroid.

Fannie Lou Hamer (*left*), Victoria Gray (*center*), and Annie Devine fought for better treatment and government representation for Black people in Mississippi.

Hamer called this the "Mississippi Appendectomy" and discovered that three out of five of all Black women in Sunflower County, where she lived, had experienced the same.

FDA Wins

Reproductive justice activists have seen quite a few successes over the years. In 1999 the US Food and Drug Administration (FDA) approved the first emergency contraceptive, or medication that can be taken after sex to prevent pregnancy. The FDA later approved a vaccine to prevent the human papillomavirus (HPV), a virus that often causes cancer.

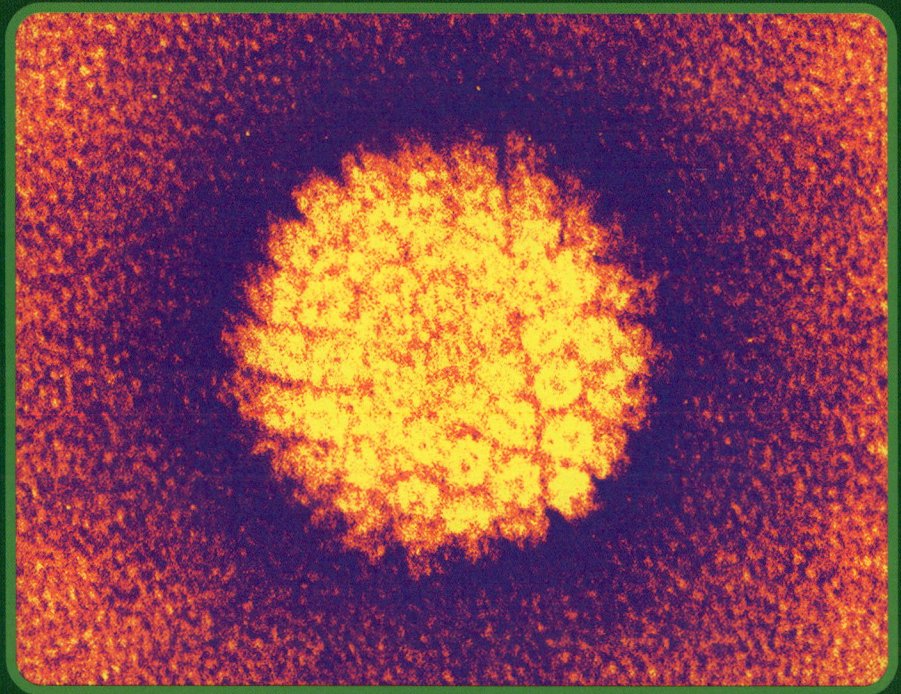

A colorized representation of HPV, a virus that can cause cancer

Forced sterilization has even happened more recently in the United States. One group that's often subjected to it is people in prison. In 2001 twenty-four-year-old California prisoner Kelli Dillon received a surprise sterilization during a different surgery. A year later, Dillon got help from a social justice legal organization to find out what really happened to her, because no one had told her the truth. The legal group also learned that more than fourteen hundred prisoners in California had been secretly sterilized from 1997 to 2013. In 2014 California passed a law intended to stop this kind of sterilization in prisons.

Birth Control

One aspect of reproductive justice is deciding for oneself whether and when to have children.

White activist Margaret Sanger grew up with ten siblings. In addition, her mother had seven miscarriages. She later died of tuberculosis. Sanger blamed her father for her mother's death, believing her mother had too many children.

Sanger later attended nursing school and became a visiting nurse on the Lower East Side of New York. There she saw many women, especially poor, immigrant women, struggling to find solutions to unwanted pregnancies. Safe medical abortions were not accessible to them, and many died after unsafe, secret abortions. As early as

Margaret Sanger in 1916

the 1910s, Sanger fought against state and federal laws that restricted women from accessing information about birth control. The Comstock Act made any writings or tools used for birth control or abortion illegal. It was even against the law for a doctor to give a patient information about family planning.

Sanger soon shifted her attention from nursing to better contraceptive and abortion options. She coined the term *birth control* in 1914 and began her quest to make sure women had more family planning options than illegal, unsafe abortions. In 1915 she was jailed for sending diaphragms through the mail. This device prevents pregnancy by acting as a barrier, stopping sperm from joining an egg. That year Sanger and other white women activists founded the National Birth Control League.

The following year, she was arrested for opening the first birth control clinic in the United States. A bit later, Sanger founded the American Birth Control League, which later became the Planned Parenthood Federation.

Birth control activism in the United States has been dominated by white women, but Black women have always been working on it too. One problem with white women being at the forefront of birth control activism is that they could put their goals into action while leaving women of color out of the conversation.

The Comstock Act

The Comstock Act of 1873 also made it illegal to send obscene or immoral publications through the mail. The act didn't define those terms, but police interpreted them widely. One male writer was even arrested after writing that women should have control over their own bodies.

Different forms of contraceptives work better for different people. Some factors that affect this are wealth, location, and access to medical care.

Poor and immigrant women often experience social issues that make their access to birth control different from wealthy citizens. People of color experience different situations as well. Structural racism is the racism in society of wealthy white people managing government, schools, and other social structures on behalf of everyone. Those patterns leave people of color and poor people with less access to good medical care and insurance. Structural racism runs so deeply and impacts many people in so many ways that it's hard to see or easily challenge it.

The Women's Political Association of Harlem

Black women of the Women's Political Association of Harlem had their first public meeting on birth control in 1918.

The eugenics mindset has also been present in birth control activism. Many historians argue that Sanger saw the women she helped as people who were not worthy of reproducing. She and others believed that birth control would be a good way to prevent "undesirable people" from having children. In the minds of eugenicists, undesirable people were usually people of color, people with disabilities, and people with less money. Sanger certainly agreed with some eugenics beliefs. For instance, she agreed that some people with disabilities should not have children. She also sometimes played into racist beliefs when she was trying to get funding from wealthy white men for birth control projects.

In the 1930s, social justice advocates pointed out that poverty, especially among African Americans, was a big problem in the South. Birth control groups traveled to the poorest parts of the South to conduct research and test different types of contraceptives. They wanted to learn which contraceptives might be cheaper and easier for poor women to use. Some reproductive health clinics had already started in these areas, but they were mostly for poor white women.

To help spread birth control access and knowledge to poor Black women in the South, Sanger and the Birth Control Federation of America launched the Negro Project. They wanted to train and pay for Black female doctors to provide knowledge and health care in Black communities. It was mostly white women who came up with this plan, and many argue that the project would be considered racist today.

The Negro Project didn't go as planned. The donors and government groups paying for it disagreed that Black communities needed their own doctors and clinics. So they changed the project to include Black women in the clinics already in place for poor white communities. But many Black people did not trust the government-funded birth control clinics to care about their needs. They wondered if the government was trying to control the Black population by providing ways to not have babies.

Margaret Sanger started the publication *the Birth Control Review* in 1917. Its goal was to share information about the growing birth control movement.

Black Women and Birth Control

While Margaret Sanger was distributing birth control and education, from the 1910s through the 1940s, several prominent Black women were working on similar health-care projects. Many of these projects included increasing the number of Black medical professionals to help support Black communities.

Activist Mary McLeod Bethune started educational initiatives. In 1904 very few schools were for Black girls, so she started one. The Daytona, Florida, school focused on skills such as sewing, teaching, and agriculture. Bethune later added a nursing program, in hopes of starting a hospital as part of the school. She spoke publicly against gender and racial discrimination in health-care policies, and President Franklin Roosevelt appointed her to his "Black cabinet," making her one of the most notable Black women of her time. As president of the National Council of Negro Women, Bethune publicly defended

Mary McLeod Bethune (*left*) worked against discrimination in health care. She had connections to important government leaders, including First Lady Eleanor Roosevelt (*right*).

birth control, notably against the powerful Catholic Church.

Dorothy Ferebee graduated at the top of her medical program in Massachusetts. But as a Black woman doctor in the 1920s, she had trouble finding an internship at the nearby white hospitals with racist policies. She moved to Washington, DC, where she finished her internship and then started her own practice and set up a childcare center to support a mostly Black neighborhood. In the

Dorothy Ferebee (*right*) worked hard to increase access to health care for women in Black neighborhoods, as well as training other Black medical professionals.

1920s, she taught obstetrics, or the study of pregnancy and birth, to medical students at the traditionally African American Howard University. Ferebee was also the medical director of the Mississippi Health Project, which visited areas of Mississippi that didn't have access to health care.

In 1941, around the same time the Birth Control Federation of America was working on the Negro Project, the National Council of Negro Women passed a resolution that supported birth control. The council was a group of clubs created by Black women that supported better housing, education, employment, childcare, and health care for Black women. The organization represented about a million women. Ferebee was its chair, and Bethune was its president.

Other Black women who worked with Ferebee to improve health care for women included E. Mae McCarroll, a doctor who worked for the department of public health and shared information on sexually transmitted diseases.

Dr. E. Mae McCarroll was born in Alabama in 1898. She later became one of the first Black doctors in the United States.

Another medical professional in their orbit was registered nurse Mabel Keaton Staupers, who fought to get Black nurses to be allowed into the American Nurses Association and led the health committee of the National Council of Negro Women.

All of these women knew that people in Black communities were more likely to trust Black health-care workers, and so they worked hard to make sure Black doctors and nurses shared information about reproductive health. They worked closely with Sanger to share reading materials, films, and medical information with groups of Black women to spread the word about their options, especially birth control.

Activists had been calling for a safe birth control pill for women for a long time. Scientific testing on such a pill started in the 1950s. But as with other medical testing, not all of this research was done safely or with consent. Some of the first people studied were patients

Planning for the Future

Access to contraceptives can change a person's life. A woman who can make decisions for herself can finish school, get and keep a good job, support herself and her family, and prepare for her children's future.

Birth Control Activist Bill Baird

Some men have been willing to fight for women's rights. In 1967 Bill Baird was arrested for handing out contraceptives to students at Boston University. Then it was legal for heterosexual married couples to access birth control. But it wasn't legal for anyone else. Five years later, Baird's case made it to the Supreme Court. That decision made it legal for unmarried people to get birth control. An activist for most of his life, Baird started a women's health clinic and was arrested eight times for lecturing on birth control.

Activist Bill Baird was arrested soon after he gave this lecture at Boston University in 1967.

at a psychiatric hospital in Massachusetts. Two hundred poor women in Puerto Rico were next, but they didn't know the medication was still in the testing stage. Early versions of the pill had big side effects, such as blood clots and throwing up.

The FDA approved the first version of the pill in 1960. But at first, only married women could get a prescription. Three years later, medical providers were prescribing the pill to 2.4 million Americans. In 1972 the Supreme Court ruled that it was legal for unmarried people to have contraceptives.

By 2019 it was estimated that fifty to eighty million women around the world have used the pill to prevent unintended pregnancies.

But many women, especially women of color, have often felt unsafe accessing contraceptives. Because they don't always trust the government or doctors, they sometimes wonder if those people have their best interests in mind. The history of eugenics in the United States has made some women wonder if the government wants them to have birth control so they won't make more children. In 1970 Black liberation activist Toni Cade Bambara published an essay discussing whether the pill was actually helpful or harmful to communities of color.

These days, women of color are still at higher risk of problems in their reproductive health than white women. Black women die in pregnancy and birth almost three times as often as white women do.

Activist Toni Cade Bambara publicly wondered if birth control pills would actually be a benefit for women of color.

Abortion Rights and *Roe v. Wade*

Roe v. Wade was a 1973 US Supreme Court case that began in Texas. The court decided that the right to privacy included the right to an abortion. But it also said that the government could make rules about when in pregnancy people could have an abortion.

Before *Roe v. Wade* made abortion legal and safe, many pregnant people found secret ways to access this medical procedure. Wealthy women often had connections to trained doctors who secretly helped women who needed it. Women with fewer resources sometimes visited less qualified "doctors" or tried to terminate pregnancies at home on their own. Many of those women ended up with infections or other health concerns, and without safe and legal medical help, many of them died.

For many years after *Roe v. Wade*, some lawmakers and people argued about when

This woman carried a sign at a 1974 rally in Pittsburgh, a year after the *Roe v. Wade* decision.

an abortion was okay. In 2022, under much political pressure, the Supreme Court overturned the 1973 *Roe v. Wade* decision.

After the 2022 decision, laws across the country were confusing for both medical providers and patients. Some

These activists in Washington, DC, rallied to support a medication called mifepristone, which can stop early stages of pregnancy.

hospitals turned away pregnant people who needed help for bleeding and other concerns because they feared that they would be arrested or that their hospitals would lose their licenses.

Some states passed laws to protect the rights to contraception and abortion. Some activists built up networks to help people in states where they couldn't get reproductive health care. Many organizations, such as the Guttmacher Institute, started tracking which states have abortion laws, so that women across the country know what their rights are.

Many people who need reproductive health care are part of communities that have historically faced discrimination, such as immigrants and people of color. When family planning is criminalized, people take matters into their own hands, which risks their safety. Others can be arrested or deported.

Still Working for Reproductive Justice

In 2021 In Our Own Voice: National Black Women's Reproductive Justice Agenda, Interfaith Voices for Reproductive Justice, SisterLove, and other groups released the *Black Reproductive Justice Policy Agenda*. This document was put together by thirty Black women's organizations and reproductive justice activists. It focuses on policy and reproductive rights issues, such as Black maternal health, reproductive health care, and access to abortions. The agenda also includes the impact of the COVID-19 pandemic upon families of color and addresses what lawmakers can do to stop the many ways that laws hurt and kill people of color. The agenda lists a number of recommendations and opportunities for partnership to create better outcomes for all.

Many organizations have taken on the fight for reproductive justice. SisterSong Women of Color Reproductive Justice Collective, or SisterSong for short, began in 1997 as a group of sixteen organizations. The collective is made up of women of color from four ethnic communities: Native American, African American, Latina, and Asian American. They work together to change policies and systems that hurt people in marginalized communities. These are people or groups that are left out because of their age, race or ethnicity, physical or mental disabilities, wealth, education level, or location.

Another national organization working on reproductive justice is In Our Own Voice: National Black Women's Reproductive Justice Agenda. They partner with other organizations to make sure that women of color are helping to lead discussions about reproductive justice.

Planned Parenthood in New York also pushes for equity in reproductive justice. The organization supports and highlights the work of the reproductive justice movement by tying in all related issues that impact a woman's right to access an abortion. For example, Planned Parenthood highlighted SisterSong's work on the lack of intersectionality in reproductive justice.

Intersectionality describes the ways that systems of inequality intersect, or build on one another. Those inequalities include gender, race, ethnicity, sexual orientation, gender identity, disability, class, and other forms of discrimination.

Activists Marcela Howell, Jessica Pinckney, and Lexi White promote contraceptive equity for Black women. Their fellowship trains students to become leaders in the movement by giving them hands-on experience in activism. They also partner with other organizations to connect with lawmakers on key issues. They work to keep local communities informed about what's happening with new laws about contraception and abortion.

Activists Lexi White (*right*) and Kris Keen (*left*) are part of a group called New Voices for Reproductive Justice. They work to improve health and well-being for Black women, girls, and gender-expansive people, or people who don't identify as male or female.

Jessica Pinckney leads a group called Access Reproductive Justice, which focuses on reproductive health care in California.

Contraceptive options are influenced by racism, gender discrimination, and education and income levels. Modern contraceptives include pills, injections or shots, and implants, or medical devices implanted in a person's body. Different contraceptives work in different ways and people's bodies are different, so individuals and their medical providers must find the ones that work best for them.

In Our Own Voices defines reproductive justice as "the human right to control our sexuality, our gender, our work, and our reproduction." And, as they point out, people can only do this if they have access to information and resources to make good choices.

Black women have always been at the forefront of activism that benefits all. Throughout history, many laws have taken access to certain rights away from women. The fight for reproductive justice continues.

IMPORTANT DATES

1907: Indiana passes the world's first forced sterilization law. The law made it legal to sterilize people in prison and psychiatric institutions. These institutions held high numbers of Black and Native American women.

1914: Margaret Sanger coins the term *birth control*.

1921: In November the First American Birth Control Conference takes place, with speakers and presentations.

1937: North Carolina becomes the first state to incorporate birth control services into a statewide public health program.

1939: Margaret Sanger and others create the Negro Project as one of the main programs within the new Birth Control Federation of America.

1941: The National Council of Negro Women passes a resolution endorsing birth control.

Mid-1950s: Clinical trials for the first birth control pill start in Massachusetts and Puerto Rico.

1960: Enovid, the first commercially available birth control pill, is approved by the FDA.

1973: The Supreme Court rules in *Roe v. Wade* that an individual person, not the government, has the right to decide whether to continue or end a pregnancy.

1983: The Supreme Court strikes down an Ohio ordinance that restricted abortion.

1990: In December the FDA approves Norplant, a contraceptive that is implanted under the skin once and can prevent pregnancy for five years.

2022: In June the Supreme Court overturns *Roe v. Wade*, taking away abortion protections.

2023: Opill, the first birth control pill in the US that does not require a prescription, is approved by the FDA.

SOURCE NOTES

13 "A New Vision for Advancing Our Movement for Reproductive Health, Reproductive Rights, and Reproductive Justice," Asian Communities for Reproductive Justice, accessed June 5, 2023, https://apirh.org/download/ACRJ_A_New_Vision.pdf.

21 Dorothy Roberts, *Killing the Black Body* (New York: Vintage Books, 1998), 90.

41 "Reproductive Justice," In Our Own Voice: National Black Women's Reproductive Justice Agenda, accessed June 5, 2023, https://blackrj.org/our-issues/reproductive-justice/#:~:text= At%20the%20core%20of%20Reproductive,a%20safe%20and%20 healthy%20environment.

SELECTED BIBLIOGRAPHY

Abrams, Abigail. "'We Are Grabbing Our Own Microphones': How Advocates of Reproductive Justice Stepped into the Spotlight." *Time*, November 21, 2019. https://time.com/5735432/reproductive-justice-groups/.

"Black Genocide." PBS, *American Experience*. Accessed June 13, 2023. https://www.pbs.org/wgbh/americanexperience/features/pill-black-genocide/.

Guerrero, Victoria. "The Black History of Reproductive Justice." Progress Texas, February 25, 2021. https://progresstexas.org/blog/black-history-reproductive-justice.

Howell, Marcela, Charity Woods Barnes, and Dazon Dixon Diallo. *Black Reproductive Justice Policy Agenda*, June 2021. https://blackrj.org/wp-content/uploads/2021/06/BlackRJPolicyAgenda.pdf.

"The Legacy of Henrietta Lacks." Johns Hopkins Medicine. Accessed June 4, 2023. https://www.hopkinsmedicine.org/henriettalacks/.

Miller, Olivia. "How Does Period Poverty Have a Negative Effect on Teenage Girls?" Global Development Commons, UNICEF, May 25, 2022. https://gdc.unicef.org/resource/how-does-period-poverty-have-negative-effect-teenage-girls.

Roberts, Dorothy. *Killing the Black Body*. New York: Vintage Books, 1997.

Schoen, Johanna. *Choice and Coercion: Birth Control, Sterilization, and Abortion in Public Health and Welfare*. Chapel Hill: University of North Carolina Press, 2005.

Walker, Jazmine. "The 50th Anniversary of Mississippi's Freedom Summer: Remembering What Fannie Lou Hamer Taught Us." Forward Together, June 2, 2014. https://forwardtogether.org/the-50th-anniversary-of-mississippis-freedom-summer-remembering-what-fannie-lou-hamer-taught-us/.

Ware, Madeleine. "Defining 'Problem Pregnancies': Religion, Medicine, and Pre-Roe Politics of Abortion in the South Carolina Clergy Consultation Service." *Journal for the Southern Association of the History of Medicine and Science* 3, no. 1 (2021). https://journals.troy.edu/index.php/JSAHMS/article/view/242.

LEARN MORE

5 Things to Know about Periods
https://kidshealth.org/en/kids/five-period.html

Henrietta Lacks Facts for Kids
https://kids.kiddle.co/Henrietta_Lacks

Menstruation Facts for Kids
https://kids.kiddle.co/Menstruation

Natterson, Cara. *The Care & Keeping of You 2: The Body Book for Older Girls*. Middleton, WI: American Girl, 2023.

Redford, Ruth. *Period: The Quick Guide to Every Uterus*. Rochester, MN: Mayo Clinic, 2023.

Tyner, Dr. Artika R. *Black Achievements in Activism: Celebrating Leonidas H. Berry, Marley Dias, and More*. Minneapolis: Lerner Publications, 2024.

INDEX

abortion, 7–8, 23–24, 35–39
Asian Communities for Reproductive Justice, 13

Bambara, Toni Cade, 34
Bethune, Mary McLeod, 29–31
birth control, 8, 12, 23–34
Birth Control Federation of America, 28, 31
birth control pill, 32
Black Reproductive Justice Policy Agenda (Howell, Barnes, and Diallo), 37
Brandford, Yanique, 15

Clayton, Eva, 11
Comstock Act, 24–25
contraceptives, 22, 24, 27, 32–34, 39–40

Dillon, Kelli, 23
disability, 19, 27, 38–39

enslaved people, 16–17
eugenics, 19, 27, 34

Ferebee, Dorothy, 30–31

Hamer, Fannie Lou, 20–21
Howell, Marcela, 39

In Our Own Voice: National Black Women's Reproductive Justice Agenda, 37–38, 41
Interfaith Voices for Reproductive Justice, 37
International Conference on Population and Development, 12

Lacks, Henrietta, 16, 18

McCarroll, E. Mae, 31
menstruation, 14
Mississippi Health Project, 31

National Birth Control League, 24
National Council of Negro Women, 29, 31–32
Negro Project, 28, 31
Norton, Eleanor Holmes, 11–12

period poverty, 14–15
Pinckney, Jessica, 39–40
Planned Parenthood Federation, 25
poverty, 27

Roe v. Wade, 35–36

Sanger, Margaret, 23–25, 27–29, 32
sexually transmitted infections, 9, 31
Sims, James Marion, 16–17
SisterSong Women of Color Rproductive Justice Collective, 38
Staupers, Mabel Keaton, 32
sterilization, 19–20, 23
structural racism, 26

Triawan, Alisha, 15

US Supreme Court, 19, 33, 35–36

Walker, Alice, 11
Waters, Maxine, 11–12
welfare, 20
White, Lexi, 39
Winfrey, Oprah, 18
Women of African Descent for Reproductive Justice, 10–11

PHOTO ACKNOWLEDGMENTS

Image credits: The Washington Post/Getty Images, pp. 2, 17, 18; Afro Newspaper/Gado/Archive Photos/Getty Images, pp. 6, 30; Mark Reinstein/Corbis Historical/Getty Images, p. 9; AP Photo/Bryan Olin Dozier/NurPhoto, p. 10; Bill Clark/CQ-Roll Call, Inc./Getty Images, p. 12; Leigh Vogel/Stringer/Getty Images Entertainment/Getty Images, p. 13; RomarioIen/Shutterstock, p. 14; Bettmann/Getty Images, pp. 21, 24, 29; Science Photo Library - PASIEKA/Brand X Pictures/Getty Images, p. 22; Science Photo Library/Getty Images, p. 26; Margaret Sanger/Wikimedia Commons PD, p. 28; Newark Library/Wikimedia Commons (CC BY-SA 4.0), p. 31; Boston Globe/Getty Images, p. 33; Peregrine/Alamy, p. 34; Barbara Freeman/Hulton Archive/Getty Images, p. 35; Probal Rashid/LightRocket/Getty Images, p. 36; NurPhoto/Getty Images, p. 39; AP Photo/Eric Risberg, p. 40. Design element: Rodin Anton/Shutterstock.

Cover: AP Photo/Bryan Olin Dozier/NurPhoto.